A
LIFE
WORTH
LIVING

LEADER'S GUIDE

Alpha

Alpha Resources
Alpha North America

For many, the Alpha Course represents the first steps in the Christian life, and many new Christians will end the course asking, "What happens next?"

A Life Worth Living is aimed specifically at those who are starting out in the Christian life and is an excellent follow-up course to Alpha.

Compiled and written by Jo Glen.

© 1999, Alpha International, Holy Trinity Brompton, Brompton Road, London SW7 1JA, UK

5 6 7 8 9 10 Printing/Year 05 04

Published in North America by Alpha North America, 74 Trinity Place, New York, NY 10006.
All rights reserved.

Text illustrations by Charlie Mackesy

ISBN 1-931808-236

Contents

Leading a Group

The primary purpose of our time talking and praying together in small groups is to help each other to draw closer to Jesus Christ. It will help this process if the three golden rules of intimacy, confidentiality, and accountability are explained regularly and adhered to.

The secondary aims are:

To discuss

To talk about issues arising out of each talk, possibly using the suggested questions arranged by chapter.

If you are leading the group, be sure to use open-ended questions, either your own or those suggested here.

You can always start by asking "Any thoughts?" or "What do you think/feel?" Then, wait. If people don't respond, nudge them a little further. Don't be tempted to answer your own question. Allow people to express their views.

Encourage those who find it hard to speak out. Be a good listener. Be well-prepared, so that you can speak with some authority if you need to, but don't wade in if you don't need to.

Always treat your group with gentleness, sensitivity, and respect.

If you don't know the answer to one of the group's questions, be honest and offer to find out before the next meeting.

Note: Groups can be ruined by:

- **weak leadership**
  not properly prepared, letting one person do all the talking.
- **overly-dominant leadership**
  doing all the talking, instead of giving people the freedom to speak and to say what is on their minds.

To pray together

Be aware that some people are not used to praying aloud and others find it very difficult.

Never force anyone. If you are the leader, keep your prayers simple so that no one feels intimidated.

As the group moves on together, the level of intimacy will increase. Meanwhile, encourage people to ask for prayer about issues in their own life, not only about world issues or their great aunt. This enables the group to get to know each other in a natural and simple way.

Feel free to ask the Holy Spirit to come and help you all in your prayers.

It may sometimes be appropriate to break into single sex groups to talk/pray about more personal or gender-specific issues.

Make it clear that a group member can ask the leader(s) to pray alone about a more personal issue.

Always introduce a new person, and be sure that everyone knows each other's names.

Do not be so rigid about the content of the discussion that you prohibit the development of friendship. It is so important that people find their place in the body of Christ. If people do not feel loved and accepted, they will not stay.

To learn to minister to one another

This is the place for people to find out about the gifts of the Spirit. Encourage each other by spotting each other's gifts and then making sure they get used.

To train others to lead

Where you see leadership potential, encourage it.

Help others grow in Christian maturity

Encourage honesty. None of us is perfect—yet.

As we allow people to be truthful about their weaknesses and struggles, we need to build an atmosphere of accountability, encouraging each other on to greater maturity in Christ.

We long to see our lifestyle reflecting our faith more and more. We know all about human weakness, but we're not going to settle for it—God's on our side and He *can* change us.

These conversations may at times be hard, but we're all in it together.

Ask people about their relationship with God, sensitively and with respect, and encourage them in their Bible reading and prayer.

Preparing a Talk

Some basic guidelines for preparing a talk based on a chapter of *A Life Worth Living*:

1. Read the Bible passage
Read the appropriate passage of Philippians carefully and prayerfully with the help of a study Bible.

2. Read the chapter of A Life Worth Living
Read the chapter of *A Life Worth Living* and watch the talk on video or listen to the talk on audio cassette. Make notes.

3. Consider who your listeners are
This will help you to make your examples as relevant as possible, and will enable you to be sensitive to the group.

4. Clarify your aim
Your general aim will be to enable your listeners to see the Bible passage in its context, and then to see how they might apply its truths to their own lives. Your ultimate aim is to see the words of the Bible bringing about change in people's lives.

5. Prepare your talk
You have plenty of material upon which to base the talk, having watched the video, read the chapter, and/or listened to the audio cassette. Each section of the talk is likely to have three levels:

a)   The meaning of the verses in Philippians in their context.

b)   A link with a contemporary example or anecdote. This may be taken from the *A Life Worth Living* video, chapter, or audio cassette, or may be one of your own.

c)   Application in listeners' lives and motivation that, with God's help, all of us can be changed.

Note that the use of your own personal examples is very effective if they are appropriate and accessible.

Keep the structure simple, and sum up in a sentence after each section.

Conclude the talk briefly and clearly.

Aim to speak for 15-20 minutes.

Practice saying the talk aloud, if possible, to a friendly critic such as a good friend or your spouse. This will enable you to see what works well and not so well, and whether the talk needs polishing.

Suggested Format for an Evening

This resource has been prepared for use with a group, probably numbering 8-15, which meets weekly or bi-monthly within a home.

Have supper together

You may choose to organize this on a rotating basis, stressing to volunteers that the meal need only be very simple. You may find that someone offers to take charge or you may decide to order take-out or pizza.

Listen to the talk on video or audio cassette

You may feel it is right to use Nicky Gumbel's talk on video or audio cassette and simply listen together each week. You may want to do this for the first week, the first few weeks, or for the whole course.

Or listen to a member of the group give a talk based on material from relevant passages in Philippians

Advice on preparing a talk based on each chapter of *A Life Worth Living* can be found on page 8.

Break for Coffee/Refreshments

Time for discussion of material and prayer

Ideas for discussion and prayer are organized chapter by chapter.

Close

Note: For the evening to work effectively, each member of the group should, if possible, read the appropriate passage in Philippians before the evening. Even if the group is watching the video or listening to the audio cassette (and no one is giving a talk), someone—probably the leader at first—needs to be responsible for preparing the evening. This would involve careful, prayerful reading of the passage, reading the appropriate chapter of *A Life Worth Living* or listening to the talk on video or audio cassette, and consideration of discussion questions.

Chapter 1
New Heart
Philippians 1:1-11

Power of God

When we hear about the events that took place in Acts 16 or the miracle of the blind man at Lake Sebu (*A Life Worth Living*, p.13), how do we feel?

Do we believe these things could happen in our own lives and experience?

Are there factors that enable the Holy Spirit to work more effectively in our lives? (The kind of things that might come out in discussion are faith, growing knowledge of Scripture, moving on in prayer, aligning one's life to the will of God, increased purity in all areas of life, recognizing the spiritual dimension to every aspect of life.)

Verse 6—What does that mean to people? How (if at all) does it affect the way we see each day of our life?

Do we have some sort of vision for our life?

Are we aware of the gifts God has given us? (This subject gives great opportunity for discussion of individual gifts, and prayer that God would use each person. Be sure that everyone present leaves the discussion knowing that they have gifts that God wants to use.)

Acts 16 – Paul and Silas had a rough time. What was their attitude about having a rough time? What is our attitude toward having a rough time? Does being a Christian guarantee an easy life?

How should we respond to difficult times? (It may be useful to point out the sufficiency of the Cross, the crucified God Jesus who suffered and suffers with us, the possibility of being refined and purified through our troubles, the perspective of eternity, great examples of godly sufferers such as Joni Eareckson Tada or Dave Dravecky, the fact that pain is inevitable but misery is a choice, the call to find joy in all circumstances. Add to all this large quantities of empathy, real practical support, and love to anyone in the group who is suffering. No one should feel condemned for being "down.")

Notes

Notes

To dwell on. Paul and Silas were prepared to risk everything—how much are we prepared to risk? Relationships? Money? Image? Friendships?

Are we willing to face the consequences of being open about our faith?

Love of God

Back to Acts 16. Look at Paul's attitude toward a) Roman authorities; b) the jailer.

In the passage in Philippians—what was Paul's attitude toward the Philippians?

The issue here is whether Christians are called to be wimps: certainly not—look how Paul stood up to Roman authorities. Also the whole area of forgiveness, not revenge—refer to Paul Negrut (*A Life Worth Living*, p. 19).

Be sure that everyone has an opportunity to be prayed for if there are people they need to forgive. This may need to be a long-term issue for some, if there is a serious history of abuse, for example. (If you feel you do not have enough experience to deal with such an issue, seek help from the leadership team at your church.)

Also look at the genuine love Paul had for the Philippians. Perhaps have a look at 1 Corinthians 13.

Having looked at these attitudes and considering 1 Corinthians 13, what difference is this going to make to our own attitudes?

Take this opportunity to pray that God would give us the eyes of Jesus as we relate to those around us.

Knowledge and Holiness

Our love of God and our love for each other are linked. In what way? How, therefore, can we become more and more effective as a home group?

Verse 9—How can we build "knowledge" and "depth of insight"?

(Point people back to the Bible; prayer; soaking ourselves in truth through Christian books, tapes, etc.; giving of ourselves in some kind of ministry, however small; asking God to help us live what we believe.)

Verses 10-11—Discerning "what is best," becoming "pure," "blameless," and "righteous."

All comes through aligning our will and our lives to the Holy Spirit.

Notes

Notes

_____

_____

_____

_____

_____

_____

_____

_____

_____

_____

_____

_____

_____

_____

_____

_____

_____

_____

_____

_____

_____

_____

_____

_____

_____

Do we really believe in the "beauty of holiness" (Muggeridge quote about Mother Teresa) or do we think a small dose of worldliness here and there, a bit of compromise, keeps us attractive?

Do we have integrity in all areas of our life?

Relationships?

Relationships with the opposite sex?

Marriage?

Money?

Work?

The way we use words?

Goals?

Our attitude toward others?

(We will come back to these issues in more detail in future chapters.)

Verse 10—"The day of Christ." Jesus is coming back sometime. We don't know when—the Father doesn't want us to know.

If you knew Jesus was coming back tomorrow, what would you change in your life? (The point of course is that we are aiming for a time when we would want to change nothing. Come, Holy Spirit, and help us!)

Chapter 2
New Purpose
Philippians 1:12-30

Advancing the Gospel

Verses 13-14—Paul was in chains, imprisoned because of his Christian faith. He used the opportunity. The palace guard were all well aware of his faith—he was chained to these guys for four hours at a time so we can be sure they knew all about Jesus!

Opportunities are everywhere

Do we use them? What opportunities do you have in a normal day to advance the Gospel?

Perhaps get into pairs and work through a normal day for each of you, writing down any opportunities you have. Note that this is not only about SPEAKING but about SERVING, LOVING, SUPPORTING, BEFRIENDING, GIVING PRACTICAL OR FINANCIAL HELP.

How can you advance the Gospel in your place of work, be it a school, an office, a shop, the home?

Notes

_____

_____

_____

_____

_____

_____

_____

_____

_____

_____

_____

_____

_____

_____

_____

_____

_____

_____

_____

Be imaginative and creative. Help each other to see new ways that God could be made visible in you and your routine.

Ask each other next week about your progress. Keep a record of how things are going in this area.

> **Leave tonight with a list of opportunities for sharing. Start using them this week.**

Paul was persecuted. Christians are persecuted all around the world.

How do we respond to that? How would we feel about living in a country where we would be persecuted for our faith?

What are we afraid of? Do we need to be afraid? (The answer is, of course, no. We need to be armed with Scripture that assures us that fear and faith are a contradiction in terms. Use this opportunity to discuss our fears openly, and to pray that God would take away these fears.)

Are we frightened of being open about our Christianity?

Is there a setting or certain people with whom we avoid mentioning our faith? Why is this? (Aim to bring fears out into the light, and pray for each other.)

Doing the right thing

Verses 15-18—These are interesting verses—quite surprising even. Paul says that the motives of Christian preachers are only a secondary concern.

To dwell on. Have people ever worried about the purity of our own motives for becoming a Christian, for joining a church, for joining a certain home group, for getting involved in a certain ministry? Many great Christians started out with wrong motives but ended up with great ministries. We are all human.

What is even more important than our motives?

(Answers should include our relationship with God, relationships with each other, our ministry, that Christ is visible in our lives and audible on our lips, our attitude toward money and possessions, etc.)

DON'T GET FIXATED ON MOTIVES, BUT START DOING THE RIGHT THING IN EVERY CIRCUMSTANCE.

Notes

Notes

The certainty of death

Verses 19-26—How do we honestly feel about death? Our own and others'?

How do we feel about heaven and hell? It may be a good idea to look at some passages on the subject: Matthew 7:13-23; 25:31-46; John 3:1-21, especially vss.13-18; and 6:35-40 (or continue to vs. 59).

We will all die. How does that affect the way we live?

How does that affect our desire to talk about our faith with people who are not Christians?

How does that affect our goals? our attitude toward money and possessions?

Pray in pairs or small groups that God would change your desires and reorder your priorities.

Living it out

Verse 27—Do we conduct ourselves in a manner worthy of the Gospel of Christ?

In our workplace?

With our acquaintances?

In our marriage?

In our friendships?

In our thought life?

In the things we read and watch?

In our habits?

With our bank accounts?

With our sexuality?

In the things we say and the way we talk about other people?

Paul talks in verse 27 about "standing firm." In what circumstances do people find it difficult to stand firm? Discuss good strategies for making progress in these areas. Pray for each other.

Paul talks about unity. Are Christians in general good at unity? Are *we* good at unity? How could we act more like a body? In which ways do my behavior, lifestyle, or standards affect you?

In what ways do our compromises have a negative effect on both Christians and non-Christians? How could we be more united as a group? How could we support each other?

Discuss practical means of mutual support. (This can be very basic, for example, baby-sitting, lending someone your car, etc.)

Notes

Chapter 3
New Attitude
Philippians 2:1-11

Some situations to dwell on!

Me First

Who do you look at first in a group photo? Yes, we are naturally self-centered.

Consider these questions:

• You are driving and a friend is following you. There is only one parking space in the lot and you arrive first. What do you do?

• (For parents.) Your child is at the age at which feeding him or her involves getting covered in food. You are at home. There is one high chair. Your friend has come over with his/her child. Who gets the high chair?

• (For prospective house buyers or tenants.) A friend of yours is looking for a house of the same price in the same area as you. You come across the perfect house. What do you do?

• (For fashion victims.) Your friend who wears the same size clothes as you has asked to borrow something for a wedding. A couple of days later, you discover you have been invited too. Who gets the best outfit?

Notes

•(For sports enthusiasts.) Three of you have been waiting in line together for tickets for a big game. You get to the booth and there are only two tickets left. Your friend went off to buy a hamburger five minutes ago and hasn't come back. What do you do?

•Someone needs a lift home from home group—you vaguely heard them mention it at the beginning of the evening. It's about 10 minutes out of your way. It's 10:50 P.M., and you're exhausted. What do you do?

•You and your friend at work are both hoping for promotions. Your boss asks for your views on your friend. How actively do you seek to commend him or her?

These could go on forever. You may be able to think of examples that apply more specifically to your group.

The point of course is: How actively do we seek to get the best for ourselves and how actively do we seek to get the best for others?

How actively do we seek to give ourselves lots of fun and an easy life and how actively do we seek the same goals for others?

This presents a great opportunity for discussion and prayer. Ultimately, the Holy Spirit will help us as we actively change. It is possible.

Notes

Notes

_____

_____

_____

_____

_____

_____

_____

_____

_____

_____

_____

_____

_____

_____

_____

_____

_____

_____

_____

We need to start changing today and being accountable for our attitudes. When we start changing, God will start to work powerfully through us.

Do we want that more than anything? Discuss the subject in pairs. Make sure you all write down areas where you want to see change.

Pray for each other in these specific areas. Enquire about each other's progress next week.

Who do we think we are?

Status

To dwell on. Do we consider ourselves to have status through our position at work or our position in the church or in society? How does our job title affect the way we see ourselves? (We don't have to admit this to the entire group—it's something to consider in our heads.)

To dwell on. Our position in the church. Do we drop this into conversations? Do we offer to talk to a certain leader on another's behalf to make ourselves feel important? (Again, for thought.)

Think of it from another angle. Do we become more interested in someone we've just met if it becomes clear that he or she is in some way "important"?

To dwell on. For those for whom things are tough. Does the fact that things are not going well for you at work or that you are unemployed or having trouble with your relationships affect the way you feel about yourself?

Make sure that everyone is reminded about God's absolutely equal and overpowering love. God is not remotely interested in our job title and there will be no job titles in heaven. God looks at all our hearts.

Pray for each other. It is very powerful for people in opposite situations to pray for each other.

Warning:

Don't be patronizing!

How can we help each other to remember that "status" and "position" are meaningless in the kingdom of God? Write down your suggestions and try to stick to them.

(Examples might be: not to ask someone what they do as a first question; treating leaders and non-leaders equally; actively seeking to make friends within church or home group who are not part of the "in crowd"; avoiding any sort of clique forming in the group.)

Rights

What rights do we have, if any? Hopefully the discussion leads to the fact that we have none. Everything we have (including the air we breathe) is a gift from God.

Notes

Notes

Jesus gave up every right, even His right to life. What a sobering thought.

Pray for each other about surrendering our rights—our right to be listened to, our right to be comfortable, our right to have certain material things, etc.

Reminder

This whole discussion has been based on the life-transforming verses of Philippians 2:1-11. Meditate on them. Pray through them. Ask God to start to imprint them on your mind and heart.

We are called to demote ourselves, to be downwardly mobile, to humble ourselves under the mighty hand of God. This is what it means to embrace the Cross.

If we exalt ourselves, God will not. If we humble ourselves, God will exalt us.

Which do we want?

Chapter 4
New Responsibilities
Philippians 2:12-18

Fulfilling our potential

Our freedom in Christ brings with it responsibilities. What are these responsibilities?

(Discussion will probably bring up our responsibility to talk about the good news of Jesus Christ with others, to develop our relationship with God and thus to keep listening to Him about the direction of our lives, to allow the Holy Spirit to transform us from within, which will lead to possibly uncomfortable changes in our lives.)

What does it mean to fulfill our potential?

(Discussion hopefully leads to the realization that we fulfill our potential when we align our will with God's and start to do the things He has called us to do. We will never fulfill our potential if we do not allow God to reveal His vision for our lives.)

Notes

We thought briefly about the deathbed perspective in Chapter 2. Consider this again.

If you were about to die, which elements of your life would seem most important?

What would you like your epitaph to be?

Have you asked God to start to talk to you about your gifts and your ministry?

We started talking and praying about this in Chapter 1. Use this opportunity for further discussion in pairs and prayer for each other.

We don't want to have a "saved soul" and a wasted life.

Just think what God might do through you in the years ahead. Ask Him to share His vision with you. Ask Him to share His vision for you as a home group.

Write down your joint and individual visions.

Getting our lives in order

Verses 14-16a—"arguing" is intellectual rebellion against God. What does this mean in practice?

(Discussion might include cynicism; diminishing God's power or love by our words; being self-sufficient and thinking *we* have all the answers, not God; etc.)

"Complaining" is essentially self-pity. How can we avoid self-pity?

(Lots of ways, but principally to take the focus off ourselves and onto others.)

Complaining is also talking negatively about the weather, our lives, our homes, our children, our friends, our husband or wife, our finances, our future, our situation.

It is okay to be realistic, but ask God for His help to see all the things we have to be thankful for. Dwell on them.

Avoid comparing any part of your life with someone else's. God deals with everyone differently. Look at examples from the Bible.

How can we avoid feeling negative?

(Discussions should lead to Bible reading and prayer, praising and worshiping God, listening to worship tapes, reading about inspiring Christians, acknowledging the thousands of people who are having a really tough time and praying for them, getting out there and doing things for others, asking God to get you passionate and envisioned for Him. Get busy for God.)

Notes

Notes

_____

_____

_____

_____

_____

_____

_____

_____

_____

_____

_____

_____

_____

_____

_____

_____

_____

_____

_____

Pray for each other and aim to say nothing negative for a whole week. It's going to be agony! Check up on each other.

"Blameless," "pure," and "shining like stars."

We need to have lives and lips with which no one can find fault.

We have looked at these things before. How are we doing?

How's our language?

How's our use of humor?

How's our attitude toward the opposite sex?

How's our attitude toward drinking?

How's our use of money?

How's our use of time?

How's our attitude toward our fellow human beings?

Have we criticized, looked down on, been rude or insensitive to anyone this week? Etc.

Keep praying for specific areas in each other's lives.

If you hadn't told them—and maybe you haven't—would all your friends, family, colleagues, and neighbors KNOW you were a Christian by looking at your life?

Use this train of thought to clarify any changes God would like you to make.

Discuss them with each other. Pray for each other. Start practicing.

Pouring ourselves out

Verses 16b-18—"running," "laboring," and "pouring ourselves out." In what ways did Paul do this? And Jesus? And us?

We have a responsibility to our church. What is it?

(Discussion should lead to the fact that we need to serve, minister, pray, and use our gifts for the good of the church and also that we need to invest time, money, and resources in the kingdom of God.)

We have a responsibility to those around us. What is it?

(Discussion again is enormous but should include thinking of ways to make our faith accessible and meaningful to those we meet, caring about every sector of society, caring about justice, etc.)

What does Paul's life teach us about sacrifice? What about Jesus—the embodiment of sacrifice?

How do you feel about the somewhat alien concept of sacrifice?

Why is it so alien to us? Do we feel there is sacrifice in our own lives?

In what way?

Notes

Notes

_____
_____
_____
_____
_____
_____
_____
_____
_____
_____
_____
_____
_____
_____
_____
_____
_____
_____
_____
_____
_____
_____
_____
_____
_____
_____

Ought there to be more? Does the way we give of our time and money, for example, involve sacrifice, or is it all quite easy and comfortable? Does that matter?

How might further sacrifice change our lives for the better or worse? Discuss concrete examples.

Chapter 5
New Friendships
Philippians 2:19-30

Being a good friend

Friendship is literally eternal. How seriously do we work at our friendships?

Take some key words from the passage for discussion.

"Genuine interest." Do we take genuine interest in each other?

Think about the home group. Have we taken the trouble to find out about each other's jobs, each other's interests, each other's anxieties, etc? If not, why not make a start?

One suggestion is to have a time each week for a different person to give a brief testimony. This helps us get to know and understand each other better as imperfect human beings with imperfect lives who are being transformed, perfected, and matured by God.

How are we to respond if a Christian friend is going wrong in some area of his or her life? What would you do if you suspected that a good friend (a

Notes

Christian) was sleeping with his or her boyfriend or girlfriend?

What if a good Christian friend told you that he or she could not afford to give at all at present?

How do we respond to requests for advice from those who would not call themselves Christians? What if a friend was intending to have an abortion?

Is it a good idea to make friends just to evangelize?

(Discussion hopefully concludes "no." We make friends out of genuine love and interest in others. The evangelism flows naturally from that.)

"As a son with his father." That's how Christian friendships should be. Could anyone in the group who is a parent expand on that? We are all someone's child, so we can contribute from that angle.

The main point about good parenting is unconditional love. How can we love our friends unconditionally? (Discussion should include forgiving them when they fail us or do something wrong.)

"Fellow worker." We who are Christians have a common vision, which can only deepen our friendship.

Does our home group have a common vision?

If not, pray toward having one. Working together for God will deepen your involvement with each other as well as your individual faith.

There is a danger in any group of friends that they become too inward-looking.

How can we prevent this home group from becoming inward-looking?

(Discussion will include getting out and serving others together.)

Pray and then discuss how to start serving others as a group. What is God calling you to do?

"Fellow soldier." Life is not always easy. How do we respond when our friends are in real difficulty—when they are depressed and unreasonable, when they have lost their job or broken up with a boyfriend or girlfriend? How can we do better?

Soldiers take risks with each other and for each other. Do we risk being open and vulnerable?

Do we respect others' openness and vulnerability by being compassionate and confidential?

If you haven't already, it may be good to reconfirm the group's commitment to intimacy, confidentiality, and accountability.

Notes

Notes

_____

_____

_____

_____

_____

_____

_____

_____

_____

_____

_____

_____

_____

_____

_____

_____

_____

_____

_____

_____

Is there anything about ourselves that we don't dare risk telling anyone?

It may be very freeing to choose someone wisely and tell them so that they can pray for you and either help you or suggest someone else who could help.

"He almost died for the work of Christ, risking his life to make up for the help you could not give me" (vs. 30). Jesus died for us. How far would we go for Him or for each other?

For thought. If we discovered one of our friends had AIDS, how would it affect our friendship with him or her?

NOTE: We cannot have the same depth of friendship with everyone. Even Jesus chose a group of 12, and had different levels of friendship within that group.

This is okay. We need to work very hard at our special friendships, while maintaining an attitude of love and integrity toward everyone we meet.

How can we guard against letting people down or disappointing them?

(Discussion should include being realistic at the beginning of a friendship, being wise by starting a friendship at the level at which we can maintain it, being honest and communicative with each other, being prayerful about our friendships, and seeking God's guidance all the time.)

How can we avoid being misleading in friendships with members of the opposite sex?

> **It is much more important to be a good friend than to find a good friend.**

Together make a list of what it means to be a true friend. The irony is, of course, that as we seek to be a good friend, we end up with good friends.

Notes

Chapter 6
New Confidence
Philippians 3:1-9

Looking at the surface

One of the points Paul was making in this passage is that circumcision was not the real issue.

What matters, he said, is to worship "by the Spirit of God." God is interested in the inside, not the outside.

We, as Christians today, are not wrestling with the issue of circumcision. What parallels can we see in our own society?

How do Christians nowadays fall into the same trap of over-emphasizing the surface at the expense of what lies underneath?

(Discussion may lead to issues such as style of worship. Of course, it doesn't matter which songs we sing or which instruments we use. What matters is that we worship "by the Spirit of God." Other issues may include doing all the religious things and working on the right committees but not being in relationship with God, etc.)

Putting our confidence in the wrong things

Most of us do this to a greater or lesser extent. Dwell on these questions—probably silently in your own heart:

What makes you feel confident when you enter a roomful of strangers or a party in full swing?

When you look back over your life, what makes you feel good about yourself?

When people you don't know ask you questions about yourself, what kind of things do you mention first?

What kind of things do you make sure people know about you? This may show what gives us our confidence.

To dwell on. How can we change? How can we convince ourselves that even if we have status, background, social class, achievements, worldly power, bank accounts, fame in our field, good looks, famous friends, an expensive car, a big house, a famous relative, a family name . . . they are all complete and utter rubbish compared to knowing Christ? Discuss.

Notes

_____

_____

_____

_____

_____

_____

_____

_____

_____

_____

_____

_____

_____

_____

_____

_____

_____

_____

_____

_____

_____

Alternatively, how can we convince ourselves that the fact that we are not famous, stunningly beautiful, immensely wealthy, obviously popular, part of the "in crowd" is of absolutely no interest to God?

What is it about us that matters to God?

Pray together and renounce wrong attitudes together. Pray for God's perspective. Pray for an inner conviction and peace that God knows what is truly important.

On your own, write a letter to God, handing over all the things that give you false and totally empty confidence. Alternatively, or also, write down some promises of God from the Bible that will remind you of how much you individually matter to God.
Suggestions: Psalm 139, Matthew 10:29-33, Romans 8: 28-39.

True Confidence

Where does true confidence come from? Discuss.

(For example, a young woman used to find it very difficult to walk into a roomful of people she didn't know. Since becoming a Christian, she prays before any event like this, and is totally transformed.

She enters the room with the confidence of Christ.)

How can we build confidence in Christ?

What does "righteousness" mean in our day-to-day lives?

(Discussion should extend to a right relationship with God and others, in every circumstance, at every minute, in every conversation, however insignificant.)

To dwell on: Secular self-esteem involves valuing oneself over and against God. Christian self-esteem involves valuing oneself in and through Christ

Notes

Notes

Chapter 7
New Ambitions
Philippians 3:10-21

What is the driving force of your life?

In you own mind, try to answer that question. What is it that directs your day today, your dreams for tomorrow, and your vision for the next 10 years?

Essentially, there are only two principal focal points to choose between. What are they? (Me or God.)

The other goals and dreams stem from one of these two. Do you agree with that? Have you made your choice? Are you finding it difficult to choose?

Friends of ours—enemies of the Cross

Paul used the term "enemies of the cross." Who are enemies of the Cross?

Do we truly believe the Bible when it says that there are two paths and two destinations? How does that change our attitude to everything?

Visible differences

There are "citizens of heaven" and there are "enemies of the cross," said Paul. We should be able to recognize who is who. How would we recognize each?

(Issues from the passage and talk should naturally flow into this discussion. The issue of "appetites"— people whose gods are eating, drinking, sensuality, sex, music, clothes, exercise, etc. Opposing values of two groups—boasting when they should be blushing, etc. Also the fact that the "citizens of heaven" should have their ultimate focus on heaven, whereas the others are inevitably restricted to the here and now—locked, blindly and tragically, into this planet and this life.)

Would it be easy to spot which we are? Are there areas where you would like God to help you change?

Body talk

What does verse 21 mean? (The answer needs to make plain that we will be given new bodies, just as Jesus was. We are not going to float around like ghosts.)

How does this make you feel?

Notes

(Answers may include the fact that it should help us deal with the passing of the years. Getting old is something that our society finds difficult to deal with, hence the obsession with cosmetic surgery and looking young. This should be an encouragement for anyone who is struggling with getting old and seeing one's body start to go downhill.)

"I want to know Christ," said Paul. Can you say that? Is it the greatest ambition of your life?

Would you like God to help it become the greatest ambition of your life? Ask Him.

"I want to *know* Christ." This is the same verb that is used to describe the way a husband knows his wife. What do you think Paul meant?

How can we begin the journey of "knowing" Christ?

(Discussion should include intimate union with Jesus and how we get there. Also, knowing the power of the Resurrection in every breath we breathe, every conversation we have, every piece of advice we give, every prayer we pray, every decision we make. We could try praying for the power of the Resurrection in our lives from the moment we get out of bed. We will struggle against sin within ourselves. In what way? We will struggle against sin in the world around us. In what way? How can we better embrace suffering? Are we willing to embrace others' suffering or do we avoid it? How can we do better in this area?)

As we strive with the help of the Holy Spirit to know Christ, we start to know our destiny.

How do you feel about heaven? Do you have assurance about the future? On what basis?

Verses 12-14—The image of the athlete. What light does that shed on the way Paul sees the Christian life?

(Discussion might include the absolute determination and single-mindedness of the athlete, the need for training and getting focused, the fact that there is a very certain destination and "prize," the need to look forward, not backward, etc.)

Notes

Notes

Chapter 8
New Resources
Philippians 4:1-9

Standing firm

Verse 1—Paul encouraged the Philippians—and us as well—to stand firm. What did he mean by that?

Dwell on this question: Where will you be in 10 years' time? (Or 20 or 30 or 40 or 50 years?)

What makes it difficult for us to "stand firm" even if that is our desire?

(Answers will probably include our fallen nature, the devil's desire for us not to stand firm, and the huge pressures of living in a godless society while trying to be godly. There's a lot against us, but all the power of the Trinity for us.)

The first part of standing firm is probably recognizing how much is against us. That will remind us of our dependence on God.

Paul went on to write about some basic foundations for life. These are highly applicable to us as Christians today.

Staying close to each other

Verses 2-3—What's going on here? Why is it that Christians don't get along with other Christians?

If we have had a falling out with another Christian, what should we do?

(Answers should include taking the initiative to reach agreement and asking for God's help to forgive, recognizing our part in the dispute, and receiving forgiveness from God as we seek to renew friendship.)

If we are aware that there has been a dispute within our own fellowship, what should our attitude be? Note what Paul says to "you, loyal yokefellow" (vs. 3).

(Answers should include helping people be reconciled and avoiding gossip or being judgmental. Note that Paul asked others to help rather than pretend the dispute hadn't happened. We can learn from that. All things must be done out of love.)

Notes

Notes

_____
_____
_____
_____
_____
_____
_____
_____
_____
_____
_____
_____
_____
_____
_____
_____
_____
_____
_____
_____
_____
_____

Staying Close to God

Three valuable tips:

1. Enjoy God

How? What should our attitude be when things are bad?

(Rejoice in God's love, mercy, promises, and presence.)

What should our attitude be when things are good?

(Check that the main reason for our joy is God. Lots of other things can add to it, but our relationship with the Lord needs to be at the center of everything.)

2. Expect God

What did Paul mean by saying "The Lord is near" (vs. 5)?

(Expect Him at any moment; He is near in His Spirit.)

Jesus could come back at any moment. How does that change the way we see things?

How can we be sure to experience and know the nearness of God?

Try to define "gentleness." What is the opposite of gentleness? (See *A Life Worth Living*, p. 98.)

3. Entreat God

What's the point of worry? Why are worry and prayer incompatible?

Can we ever truly avoid worry in our life? If so, how? (The answer should be yes, that's what we're working toward with the help of God. We avoid worry by staying close to God in every aspect of our life, and by bringing absolutely every anxiety to Him in prayer.)

To dwell on. Do you feel you know the "peace of God"? Is there anything preventing you from knowing this peace?

(This could include unconfessed sin, wrong relationships, lack of time spent with God, not reading the Bible, not praying, etc.)

Pray for each other.

What is really going on in your mind?

Which of these matters the most— what we think about, what we do, what we say, or what we have?

(The Bible says that our thoughts are the most important because they affect all the others. See Matthew 15:19-20.)

If unhelpful thoughts enter our minds, what can we do to stop them?

Notes

_____

_____

_____

_____

_____

_____

_____

_____

_____

_____

_____

_____

_____

_____

_____

_____

_____

_____

_____

_____

_____

_____

Notes

(The minute one appears, say no to it in the name of Jesus, and ask for God's help to entertain it no longer. Then quickly focus on God's truth, a Bible verse, some worship music, something great God has done for you, your vision for your life, your desire to serve God in the next minute and always, etc.)

The first and last thoughts of the day are important. How can we begin and end the day well?

Our thought life is vital to our well-being as a Christian. It is like the keel of a yacht or the foundation of a house.

If anyone is struggling with their thought life, they should be encouraged to seek someone wise with whom to chat and pray this through.

Good role models

To dwell on. Are you a good role model to other Christians?

If a less mature Christian modeled himself or herself on you, would it be beneficial to them?

Note that the way we think, act, and talk has an impact on others' faith. How can we be responsible in this area?

Note that Paul was not ashamed to put himself forward as an example of a life to be followed.

Have you been inspired by another Christian in any area of your life such as family life, marriage, friendship, prayer life, faith? What effect has this had?

Get on with it!

Paul has spoken about avoiding quarrels, about avoiding worry, about filling one's mind with good things, about being inspired by other godly people. Now he says: "Put it into practice!"

If we are serious about our Christian life, the time for talk is over.

Pray for each other and get started!

Notes

Chapter 9
New Generosity
Philippians 4:10-23

Money and possessions

Write down your three most treasured possessions. Consider how easy it would be to give one or all of them away.

It may be worth writing a letter to God at some point listing all your treasured possessions and giving them back to God.

How about actually giving one or some or all of them away? Freedom!

Whether you have a lot of money or not much, how do you think God would like you to see your money?

How does God see your money?

Why has God given us our money?

For thought: Do you ever use your money and possessions to draw attention to yourself?

For thought and discussion: Would God like for you to change any of the ways you use your money? How would you feel about submitting your budget to the scrutiny of a friend? Think about doing so. Or at least keep a record of your spending for a while and think about what God would think of it.

If you earn a lot of money, how would you feel if your salary dropped dramatically? (This is a question for thought, unless your group is very intimate.)

If you earn very little, how would you feel if you became wealthy? (Again, this is a question for thought, unless your group is very intimate.)

What are the advantages and disadvantages of either situation?

(This should lead to a discussion about the heavy responsibility of wealth as a Christian; good stewardship; the difficulty we can experience when we are called to be generous with large sums of money; the temptations of wealth—it can be much harder to have true faith when you are wealthy; money can be an obstacle in our faith; money can be a great blessing to others [it is more blessed to give than to receive]; money often makes life a lot easier on the surface though it may not lead to happiness, etc.)

How easy would it be to play the lottery with the promise that if you won the jackpot you would give it all away? Discuss!

Notes

Notes

_____

_____

_____

_____

_____

_____

_____

_____

_____

_____

_____

_____

_____

_____

_____

_____

_____

_____

_____

Is it okay to save?

Do we still give when we are in need ourselves?

End this section with the fact that the only rule in the New Testament is generosity and love in everything.

Why should we give?

Why should we give any of our hard-earned money away?

(Discussion should lead to the three points that giving blesses the recipient, the giver, and God.)

Why is giving so alien to today's Westerner?

(Look at the rise of capitalism, individualism, and materialism.)

We're always telling our children to share. How good are we at sharing? How can we get better at sharing?

Make some strategies for ways to share your money, your possessions, your time, your home, and your gifts.

Read Acts 20:35 and 2 Corinthians 9:6-7. Do we believe this?

Does anyone have an example from their own life when their giving of anything—not just money—has very obviously led to them being blessed?

Jesus made the perfect sacrifice for us on the cross. We need to remind ourselves that sacrifice is part of the Christian life.

Have you started to include sacrifice in your life since the subject came up last time?

How is it that giving our money away liberates us? Try it. Be as absolutely generous as you can this week and see how it affects your life. Report back next week.

Pray for each other—that God would give you His thoughts on the subject of giving and would release you into new levels of generosity.

Final thoughts

As we conclude this course, what have we learned about Christian life?

What do we especially want to remember and put into practice?

What is the essence of Christianity in your view?

What is it that truly makes life worth living?

Notes

Other Resources

Alpha books by Nicky Gumbel:

Questions of Life

The Alpha Course in book form. In 15 compelling chapters the author points the way to an authentic Christianity that is exciting and relevant to today's world.

Searching Issues

The seven issues most often raised by participants of Alpha: suffering, other religions, sex before marriage, the New Age, homosexuality, science and Christianity, and the Trinity.

Challenging Lifestyle

An in-depth look at the Sermon on the Mount (Matthew 5—7). The author shows that Jesus' teaching flies in the face of modern lifestyle and presents us with a radical alternative.

The Heart of Revival

Ten Bible studies on the Book of Isaiah, drawing out important truths for today by interpreting some of the teaching of the Old Testament prophet Isaiah. The book seeks to understand what revival might mean and how we can prepare to be part of it.

30 Days

Nicky Gumbel selects 30 passages from the Old and New Testaments which can be read over 30 days. It is designed for those taking the Alpha Course and others who are interested in beginning to explore the Bible.

For more information on Alpha, including details of tapes, videos, and training manuals, contact one of the following.

Alpha U.S.A.
74 Trinity Place
New York, NY 10006
Tel: 888.949.2574
Fax: 212.406.7521
e-mail: info@alphausa.org
www.alphausa.org

Alpha Canada
1620 W. 8th Ave, Suite 300
Vancouver, BC V6J 1V4
Tel: 800.743.0899
Fax: 604.224.6124
e-mail: office@alphacanada.org
www.alphacanada.org

To purchase resources in Canada:

Cook Communications Ministries
P.O. Box 98, 55 Woodslee Avenue
Paris, ONT N3L 3E5
Tel: 800.263.2664
Fax: 800.461.8575
e-mail: custserv@cook.ca
www.cook.ca

Notes

Notes

Notes

Notes

Notes

Notes

Notes